SOUTHEND-ON-SEA TRAMWAYS

Robert J Harley

MP Middleton Press

First published April 1994

ISBN 1 873793 28 6

© *Middleton Press 1993*

Design - Deborah Goodridge

Published by Middleton Press
            Easebourne Lane
            Midhurst
            West Sussex
            GU29 9AZ
        Tel: (0730) 813169
(From 16 April 1995 - (01730) 813169)

Printed & bound by Biddles Ltd,
        Guildford and Kings Lynn

CONTENTS

INTRODUCTION AND ACKNOWLEDGEMENTS

This is the first Tramway Classics volume to feature a tramway system north of the River Thames. My thanks go to both George Gundry and John Price who have contributed research material, photographs and personal reminiscences. Other valuable views are from W.A.Camwell, C.Carter, R.Elliott, D.W.K.Jones, S.E.Letts, J.H.Meredith, M.J.O'Connor, D.A.Thompson and the collections of C.F.Klapper, C.L.Rayner and R.Sims. I must also thank the Essex County Record Office at Chelmsford. Rosy Thacker and Glynn Wilton of the National Tramway Museum deserve medals for all the help and time spent in assisting me in this project. I have consulted books by V.E.Burrows and Richard Delahoy together with the series of articles written for Tramway Review in 1964 by R.C. Anderson, who also penned a history of the pier tramway which was published in Modern Tramway in 1965. The rolling stock survey is based on material by Walter Gratwicke now preserved at the library of the National Tramway Museum. Tickets have been supplied by G.Croughton.

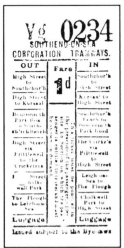

GEOGRAPHICAL SETTING

Situated in the county of Essex on the north bank of the estuary of the Thames, Southend-on-Sea is built on a ridge of land which rises from the shore to a height of over 100 feet above sea level. The Ordnance Survey maps are to the scale of 25" to 1 mile and are from the 1922 edition.

HISTORICAL BACKGROUND

The Thames estuary has seen many comings and goings during recorded history; the Romans and subsequent Saxon invaders used the river as a means of trade and later settlement. The villages of Leigh and Prittlewell pre-date the establishment of Southend and it was the arrival of the London, Tilbury and Southend Railway in 1854 which sparked development of the town as a dormitory to London and as a holiday resort. Previous to this date, a pier had been constructed in 1830 to cater for steamer traffic and it was extended to the deep water channel in 1846. The mile long structure was a European record holder at the time, and its convenience was further enhanced by the inauguration of a narrow gauge horse tramway in 1851, which was electrified in 1890 using a conductor rail system. On the landward side, the need for public transport in the rapidly expanding town was met by the construction of Southend-on-Sea Light Railways, a 3ft. 6ins./ 1067mm. gauge electric tramway equipped with overhead wires. Lines were opened on 19th July 1901 from High Street (Middleton Hotel) to Leigh and Southchurch with a branch from the Great Eastern Railway station to the Beach via Southchurch Avenue. Prittlewell was linked to the High Street by a circular service running by way of North Road and Victoria Avenue. At that time many of the thoroughfares used by the tramways were little more than country lanes.

On 1st July 1905, Robert Birkett was appointed as new manager and under his regime the tramways were expanded and modernised to meet the new transport demands of residents and trippers. In August 1908 the tracks reached a new terminus at Bryant Avenue on the seafront; the next year the service was extended to "Halfway House" and Thorpe Hall Corner. Thorpe Bay was reached in February 1912. Unfortunately the Prittlewell route was losing money, therefore, the decision was taken to cut back the track to the entrance of North Road, Prittlewell in

January 1912; the section on North Road to the "Cricketers" was abandoned and the track lifted. A plan was conceived to bring coal by sea to the loading pier on the front and to transport it by specially built trams to the generating station by the depot. Three coal trams were delivered and the service started in 1915.

On the eastern side of the town an imaginative highways and housing policy included the construction of tree lined boulevards with double tramtrack on private right of way. Bournes Green was reached in 1913 and a circular tour was at last possible with the opening of Thorpe Boulevard to connect with the sea front tracks in July 1914. After World War I the corporation started to renovate the fleet; windscreens and enclosed top decks were added to many cars. On the debit side, the rump of the Prittlewell service was converted to trolleybuses in 1928. Further trams were purchased secondhand from Middlesbrough and Accrington in 1934; both sets of cars had to be regauged to run on Southend tracks. Inspite of this renewed purchasing activity the writing was on the wall for the trams and the first closure of the general abandonment programme was the section along the boulevards from Southchurch to Thorpe Bay in July 1938. Kursaal to Thorpe Bay went over to trolleybuses in June 1939, but the intervention of the Second World War postponed the end of the system until 8th April 1942 when the last car entered the depot in London Road.

The pier tramway survived the wartime hostilities and was equipped with new rolling stock in 1949; it continued to perform a valuable role in the town's transport. In July 1976 fire destroyed the pierhead extension. The tramway was closed completely in October 1978 and the rolling stock was scrapped. However, the pier was subsequently repaired and a new single line with diesel trains was opened in 1986.

Week-Days.
Leigh Section.

High Street to Leigh.—5.5, 5.30, 6.0, 6.30, 6.33, 6.55, 7.15, 7.25, 7.35, 7.45, 7.52, 8.0, and every six minutes to 9 a.m., then every five minutes to 4.0 p.m., then every three minutes to Chalkwell Park, and every six minutes to Leigh to 9.0 p.m., then from 9.0 p.m. to finish every five minutes to Leigh.

Leigh to High Street.—5.30, 6.0, 6.30, 6.50, 7.0, 7.20, 7.40, 7.50, 8.0, 8.10, 8.17, 8.24, 8.30, and every six minutes to 9.30 a.m., then every five minutes to 4.30 p.m., then every six minutes to 9.30 p.m., then every five minutes to finish.

Thorpe Bay and Beach Section.

High Street to Thorpe Bay.—5.0, 5.40, 6.10, 6.30, 7.0, 7.15, 7.30, 7.40, 7.55, 8.5, 8.17, 8.30, 8.45, 8.55, 9.7, 9.18, 9.25, and every ten minutes to finish.

Thorpe Bay to High Street.—5.20, 6.5, 6.30, 6.52, 7.17, 7.37, 7.47, 7.57, 8.12, 8.22, 8.35, 8.47, 9.0, 9.12, 9.25, and every ten minutes to finish.

Bournes Green Section.

High Street to Bournes Green.—5.22, 5.55, 6.20, 6.45, 7.35, 7.50, 8.0, 8.10, 8.20, 8.30, 8.40, 8.50, 9.0, and every 15 minutes to finish.

High Street to Southchurch.—5.10, 5.22, 5.55, 6.20, 6.45, 7.10, 7.25, 7.35, 7.40, 7.50, 8.0, 8.15, 8.30, 8.40, 8.50, 9.0, and every 7½ minutes to finish.

Bournes Green to High Street.—5.37, 6.7, 6.32, 6.57, 7.57, 8.10, 8.20, 8.35, 8.48, 9.0, 9.10, 9.21, and every 15 minutes to finish.

Southchurch to High Street.—5.20, 5.40, 6.10, 6.35, 7.0, 7.25, 7.40, 7.50, 8.0, 8.15, 8.25, 8.38, 8.55, 9.5, 9.18, and every 7½ minutes to finish.

Prittlewell Section.

High Street to Prittlewell.—5.5, 6.10, 7.50, 8.0, and every 10 minutes to finish

Prittlewell to High Street.—5.15, 6.20, 8.0, and every 10 minutes to finish.

Sundays.

Leigh Section.—From 10.0 a.m. to finish, every five minutes.

Thorpe Bay and Beach Section.—From 10.0 a.m. to finish, every six minutes.

Bournes Green Section.—From 10.0 a.m. to finish, every nine minutes.

Prittlewell Section.—From 10.0 a.m. to finish, every 10 minutes.

Fares.

Leigh Section.—Between High Street and Chalkwell Park Gates, 1d.; between "The Plough" and Leigh-on-Sea, 1d.; between High Street and Leigh-on-Sea, 2d.

Southchurch and Beach Sections.—Between High Street and Southchurch, 1d.; between High Street and Camper Road, 1d.; between Luna Park and Thorpe Hall Avenue, 1d.; between Southchurch and Luna Park, 1d.; between High Street and Half-way House, 1½d.; between Southchurch and Half-way House, 1½d.; between Bournemouth Park Road and Half-Way House, 1d.; between High Street and Thorpe Hall Avenue, 2d.; between Bournemouth Park Road and Thorpe Hall Avenue, 1½d.

Prittlewell Section.—Between High Street and Vicarage Corner, ½d.

VICTORIA CIRCUS / WARRIOR SQ. TRACK LAYOUT IN 1921 (NOT TO SCALE)

VICTORIA AVE.

GARONS CORNER

MC

DIXONS CORNER

SOUTHCHURCH RD.

HOTEL VICTORIA

SC

HIGH STR. BROADWAY

WARRIOR SQ.

TRAMS TRAVERSE WARRIOR SQ. ANTICLOCKWISE

OVERHAUL WORKS

P.S

PS = PAINT SHOP

EASTWOOD BLVD.

CAVENDISH GARDENS

GROVE

FAIRFAX DRIVE

PRITTLEWELL

VICTORIA AVE.

WEST STR.

NELSON

NELSON RD.

WELLINGTON AVE.

SOUTHBOURNE GROVE

NORTH RD.

Y

B
B

SWEY

TRACK X..Y ABANDONED 1917

LONDON ROAD

TRAM DEPOT TRACK LAYOUT (NOT TO SCALE)

STATION RD.

LEIGH ROAD WEST

LEIGH RD.

C

C

CHALKWELL PARK

C

LONDON ROAD

COTSWOLD RD.

PLOUGH HOTEL

SHEPHERD'S COT

LONDON ROAD

C

HAMLET CT.

KINGS ROAD

CHALKWELL AVENUE

X

CRICKETER'S HOTEL

LEIGH BROADWAY

C

GRAND DR.

ST CLEMENT'S CHURCH

CHALKWELL STN.

1901-08 ORIGINAL LAYOUT AT CRICKETER'S HOTEL

WESTCLIFF STN.

L.M.S.

WESTERN

NORTH STATION

LIMIT OF COVERED TRACK AT PILE 18.

PIER TRAMWAY TRACK DIAGRAM AS AT 1965 (NOT TO SCALE)

SC = SCISSORS CROSSOVER

SC

SC

NORTH SIGNAL CABIN AT PILES

SOUTH SIGNAL CABIN AT PILES

RIVE

PIERHEAD

SOUTH STATION PILES 217 - 225

1. Leigh - Warrior Square

1. A bright summer's day greets us at the Leigh terminus of the Southend tramways. St.Clement's Church, pictured here, was described in a turn of the century guide book as,"built in later Perpendicular style with fine tower on the west and spacious brick porch of the Tudor style." Car 2 adds a touch of modernity to this 1901 scene. (Tramway and Railway World)

2. Still in the early days of the tramways, we observe a group of children, some of whom are barefoot, whilst car 17 with a full top deck including ladies with their parasols, rumbles eastwards in the direction of Southend town centre. The clock on the bracket arm has been set to indicate the next departure.
(R.J.Harley Coll.)

3. The store in the background still survives. Car 24 in its final condition waits for some of the traffic to clear before reversing in 1938. (W.A.Camwell)

4. Car 66 at Leigh terminus; the motorman will shortly change ends and gradually ease the tram in the direction of car 60 waiting further down the Broadway. The trolley pole will then gently take the right hand wire using the reversing triangle to resume its trailing position to the direction of travel.
(D.A.Thompson)

5. A fine view of car 44 on a warm day with the top saloon windows open. We are looking north and the date is 20th August 1939; in less than two weeks the country would be plunged into the Second World War.
(D.A.Thompson)

6. Some of the impact of wartime can be noted in Leigh Broadway on a February day in 1942. Both trams have headlamp masks with a white stripe on the dash to aid visibility in the blackout. Several shops are boarded up and they will have to wait another three years for the return of peace and the holiday crowds. (W.A.Camwell)

7. A final backward look at St.Clement's Church. Note the phantom pair of legs on the corner of Victoria Road! Obviously not everyone wanted to remain still for the photographer. The picture was taken before a start was made in 1910 on doubling the track between Southchurch and Leigh. (G.L.Gundry Coll.)

8. Broadway looking west, Leigh-on-Sea is the caption for this commercial view. The narrow track gauge of 3ft. 6ins. accentuates the slender nature of the double deck tramcar. The overhead here was arranged for swivel head trolleys which were commonly used in Britain and France; this method presented a neater appearance than the system used for fixed head trolleys and pantographs where the wires had to stay close to the centre line of each running track. (G.L.Gundry Coll.)

9. Outside the Grand Hotel, Leigh, car 17 looks spotless in its polished dark, olive green livery; the corporation coach painters would allow four weeks for a thorough repaint of each car, the thinking being that another paint job would not be needed for around another ten years. The crew of conductor Lambert and driver Lee are also smartly turned out in white topped caps for the summer season of 1913. (J.H.Price Coll.)

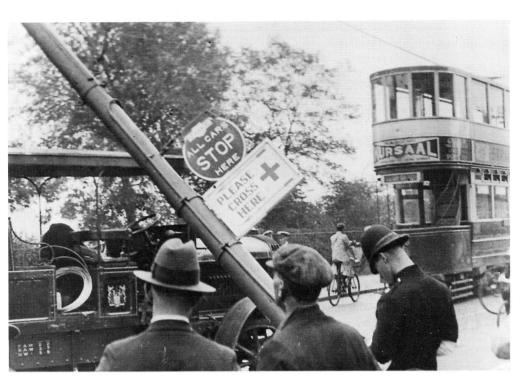

11. A spot of bother at Chalkwell Park as a PC notes down "particulars" concerning the traction standard which has draped itself gracefully across a corporation tower waggon. The philosophy of "the service must go on" is illustrated by car 48 on its way to Leigh. (G.L.Gundry Coll.)

10. Leigh was once a fishing village renowned for its brown shrimps and its connection with a famous nautical dynasty sporting the apt surname of Haddock which supplied the Royal Navy with no less than two admirals and seven captains. The upper town through which this tram is passing evolved rather less romantically to cater for holidaymakers and commuters to London. (C.Carter)

12. At the junction of London Road and Hamlet Court Road car 1 passes fully loaded. The date is around 1904. On the left is the Shepherd's Cot. (G.L.Gundry Coll.)

13. Car 21 leaves the passing loop opposite The Cot. The photographer is stationed on the top deck of a tram going in the other direction. (J.H.Price Coll.)

Ra6196 SOUTHEND-ON-SEA CORPORATION TRAMWAYS		
OUT	FARE	IN
Southchurch	1D	Bournemouth Pk. Road
Luna Park		
Half-way House		Luna Park
Thorpe J Ave.		
Frittlewell		The Plough
Chalkwell Park Gates		
Leigh-on-Sea		High Street
Luggage		Luggage
Issued subject to the Bye-laws		

Fl 6636 SOUTHEND-ON-SEA CORPORATION TRAMWAYS.		
OUT	Fare	IN
High Street to Southchurch	1D.	Southchurch to High Street
High Street to Kursaal and Beach		Kursaal and Beach to High Street
High Street via Prittlewell to the Cricketers		The Cot'e to via Prittlewell to High Street
H Street to Chalkwell Park		Leigh-on-Sea to The Plough
The Plough to Leigh-on-Sea		Chalkwell Park to High Street
Luggage		Luggage
Issued subject to the bye-laws		

15. Car sheds were rarely visited by the general public and it was left to dedicated transport photographer W.A.Camwell to record this depot scene. Cars 15, 28 and 26 are seemingly "hors de combat" awaiting their imminent demise at the hands of the breakers. Trolleybus 122 is a newer vehicle built as a one-off by the Gloucester RCW Co and acquired for the sum of £950 in 1934. (W.A.Camwell)

14. The entrance to the depot on London Road sees a group of tramway enthusiasts surrounding car 60 which had been hired by the Light Railway Transport League for a farewell visit on Sunday 8th February 1942. (G.L.Gundry)

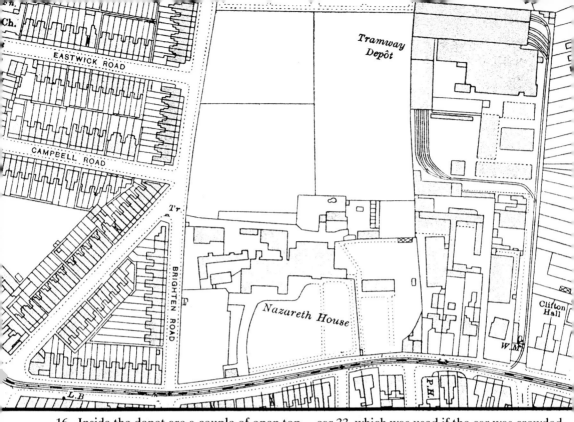

16. Inside the depot are a couple of open top cars; the indicator of the leading tram has been turned to show Prittlewell, a service which disappeared some years before this photo was taken in 1938. Note the cleaners' gantries and the unpaid fares box on the front bulkhead of car 33, which was used if the car was crowded and the conductor was not able to collect a fare before the passenger alighted. It is not recorded how many travellers were honest enough to avail themselves of this facility! (W.A.Camwell)

17. We reach Victoria Circus at the heart of the Southend-on-Sea tramways. In August 1939 car 67 slows before traversing the junction pointwork. (D.A.Thompson)

18. A fine picture taken outside Dixons. Car 58 pauses to let a motor coach slip past; note that the tram is drawing power from the trolleybus overhead. (C.F.Klapper)

19. Three forms of road traction seen together in the town centre; car 25 and the Garrett built trolleybus of 1929 (right). Both were scrapped in 1939. Southend's experimental trolleybus of 1925 brought the wires down in Victoria Circus six times during the first month of operation; needless to say, the opinions of the overhead linesmen regarding the newfangled "trackless" were somewhat pointed!
(National Tramway Museum)

20. Looking south at Dixons Corner, Victoria Circus, the conductor helps a passenger board a car heading for Southchurch, while an Austin 10 is forced to wait. (R.J.Harley Coll.)

21. An unusually deserted scene as another Garrett trolleybus heads north to Prittlewell whilst two trams pause outside a shuttered Dixons. The whole atmosphere suggests a Sunday in winter. (C.L.Rayner)

22. A pre-opening scene at Victoria Circus as everything is tested ready for the big day. (Tramway and Railway World)

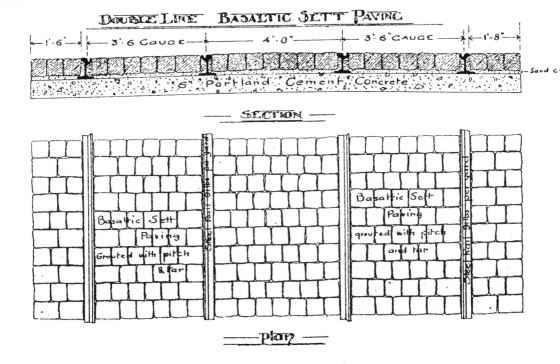

DOUBLE LINE — BASALTIC SETT PAVING

1'·6" | 3'·6" GAUGE | 4'·0" | 3'·6" GAUGE | 1'·8"

6" Portland Cement Concrete — Sand cu

— SECTION —

Basaltic Sett Paving Grouted with pitch & tar

Basaltic Sett Paving grouted with pitch and tar

— Plan —

23. Tracklaying in 1901 with Dixons on the right and the splendid covered entrance to Hotel Victoria to the left. All work of this nature was done manually in those days and hard graft was the order of the day. No doubt, the workmen welcomed the brief respite to pose for the camera. (J.H.Price Coll.)

24. Shortly after the opening of the service, cars 2 and 9 proudly display their original livery of very pale green waist panels and stair stringers which contrast with the dark green dashes and rocker panels. (G.L.Gundry Coll.)

25. A triumphal archway of traction standards and street lamps greets the arrival of two tramcars in this High Street scene just south of Victoria Circus. The cylinder hanging in the centre of the picture is a self adjusting arc light, known as a Jablachkoff candle. (R.Sims)

26. The original terminus in High Street is featured here with a car loading for Leigh. (G.L.Gundry Coll.)

27. The crowds have gone from the terminus leaving the road clear for this shot of the lower deck of car 15 complete with motorman and conductor. For those readers unfamiliar with the workings of a tramcar, the motorman's left hand is on the controller handle; this regulated the current to the motors. His right hand grips firmly the handbrake handle which was turned to apply the brakes. (R.Sims)

28. In 1921 new tracks were laid in Warrior Square to alleviate the traffic congestion in High Street. Car 60 is seen here standing on the scissors crossover whilst taking part in the LRTL tour of 8th February 1942. (C.Carter)

29. Warrior Square again on the bleak, sad farewell tour. As this was wartime, all photographers were looked upon with some suspicion and we can only assume that local fears were allayed by the appearance of many of the tram afficionados who were in military uniform. (C.Carter)

←

30. Brighter days, as the sun shines down on car 44 and its crew positioned in Warrior Square during the summer of 1924. The bell hanging next to the driver was rung vigorously to warn others straying on to the tram tracks; many a holiday crowd was cleared in this way, some folk reacted quickly without turning round thinking they were being pursued by a fire engine! In those days most other tramways used gongs and the emergency services, fire, police and ambulance used bells. (R.Sims)

31. We are now looking east and the tramway waiting shelter seems bereft of regular passengers; only the 1942 tram tour participants look somewhat stoically towards the camera. The dogged determination and "we'll see it through" attitude is manifest in the expressions. (W.A.Camwell)

32. Trams normally ran anti-clockwise round the Warrior Square loop and a conductor casts a sideways glance as car 11 moves off back to Leigh. The destination board on the waist panel was lettered in black on an ivory background. (Dr.H.Nicol)

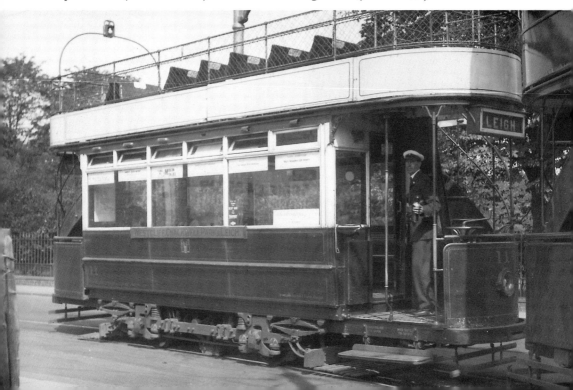

2. Victoria Circus - Prittlewell

33. At the hub of the system in front of the imposing Technical School building, later the Municipal College, a rather temporary looking shed serves as a paying in hut before a more permanent cash office kiosk could be built. (J.H.Price Coll.)

34. At the corner by the Blue Boar Hotel a tram turns into West Street, Prittlewell. (J.H.Price Coll.)

35. Outside the Blue Boar car 14 pauses with apparently only a couple of fare paying passengers on board. In May 1921 this location became the terminus and the remaining track in West Street and North Road was abandoned. (R.Sims)

36. Car 4 negotiates the points in West Street; it has just passed the entrance to Roots Hall, home of Southend United FC. The admission for a game in season 1914-15 was sixpence (2p); ladies, soldiers in uniform and boys were half price! (G.L.Gundry coll.)

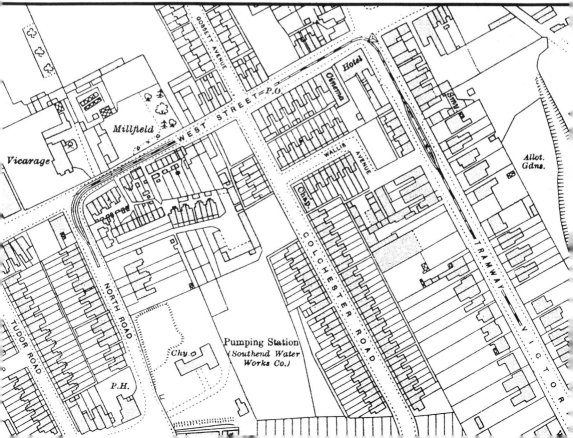

3. Kursaal - Thorpe Bay

37. Due to petrol rationing it was perfectly safe to stand in the roadway next to car 60. The board behind the belisha beacons points along Southchurch Avenue towards the Kursaal; the wiring over the tracks going to Southchurch via Southchurch Road has already been dismantled. (W.A.Camwell)

38. Looking seawards down Southchurch Avenue, we can glimpse the outline of what was then Luna Park, later to become the Kursaal. A tram glides up the hill passing a horse drawn char-a-banc.
(Tramway and Railway World)

39. The German word Kursaal suggests the more genteel world of taking the spa waters, rather than the boisterous setting of Southend sea front. However, Kursaal it remained, and the amusement centre covering some 18 acres become a local landmark. Here we see one of the early 1-10 series cars picking up passengers outside the main entrance. (J.H.Price Coll.)

40. Car 20 halts outside the Kursaal. This tram was used to transport council members and Board of Trade officers on the completion of the boulevard routes on 16th July 1914. The motorman on that occasion was Mr.Rayner. (G.L.Gundry Coll.)

41. "Dinners, Teas, Ices" proclaims the placard as a 1930s visitor in the shape of ex-Accrington, now Southend car 67, waits for customers. (R.J.Harley Coll.)

42. Car 37 displays its municipal pride with "County Borough Of Southend-On-Sea" picked out in gold shaded letters on the rocker panel. (National Tramway Museum)

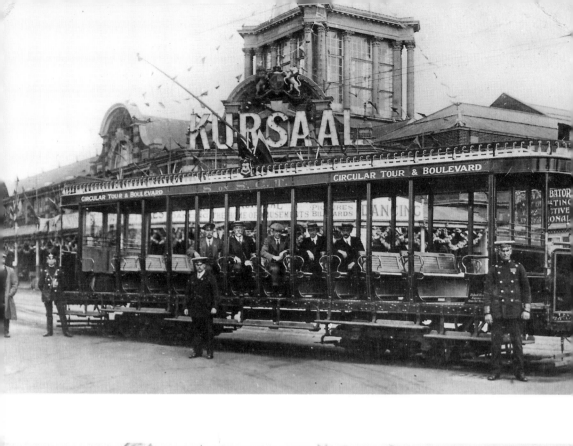

43. The famous circular tour began operations on 1st August 1914 just before the outbreak of World War I. Car 41 would normally be loaded with happy trippers intent on a good day out by the seaside; this gloomy looking group don't seem to have got into the spirit of things. (J.H.Price Coll.)

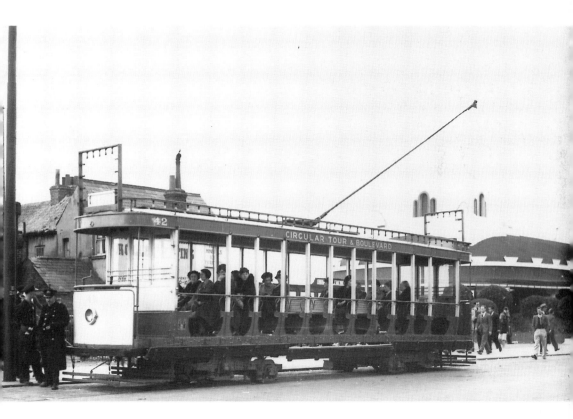

45. Car 42 stands at the Kursaal siding a short time before the end of the service in 1938. The novelty of a trip round the town on a toastrack tram had waned somewhat. (W.A.Camwell)

44. The lad standing on the step board of car 40 is one of the trolley boys employed on the circular tour cars to assist the conductor and to warn passengers not to lean out when the car passed close to some large trees on the boulevards. Note the loading barriers to cope with the seasonal crowds; the fare right round was sixpence. (R.Sims)

46. Car 28 was a very traditional, basic British open top tram of the sort that ran in many towns and cities. Here it gathers speed past the Minerva Hotel; the route board on the side of the car had a red background with white letters. (C.Carter)

47. Car 13 had a pedigree stretching back to 1904 when it was originally numbered car 11. It underwent extensive rebuilding in its Southend career; it still seems smart and well maintained in this picture. It was scrapped in 1937. (C.Carter)

48. The bracing sea air wafts over the holiday-makers as a rather weary white jacketed conductor rests his head. He is sharing the rear platform with a child's pushchair. Note the steps are in the folded position and as a further precaution, a bar across each seat entrance prevents unauthorised boarding or descending from the car. (M.J.O'Connor)

49. The tracks reached Halfway House in June 1908 and this card which was posted in August 1910 shows the provisional terminus. The full section to Thorpe Bay was opened in May 1911. (G.L.Gundry Coll.)

50. Along Thorpe Esplanade the double tracks were offset on the seaward side of the road. Car 36 has Luna Park on the destination box. (R.J.Harley Coll.)

51. Not what one would call an orderly queue! This is the scrum eager to get on at the Thorpe Bay terminus which was the end of the line from May 1911 to July 1914 and again from July 1938 to abandonment in May 1939. Those interested in social trends may wish to study the fashions of the period; certainly anyone going "topless" on the beach in those days would have been immediately arrested and incarcerated! (G.L.Gundry Coll.)

52. Hemlines have risen in this 1922 view and the conductor is on the top deck about to swing the trolley pole. (G.L.Gundry)

53. Car 63 has the front to itself as it approaches the curve to take it inland along Thorpe Hall Avenue. (W.A.Camwell)

55. The stop sign informs visitors of the tram services as car 66 edges out on to the sea front in this 1938 scene. (W.A.Camwell)

54. We glance inland to catch sight of car 22; from the state of the dash it would seem to have taken a few bumps recently. (R.Elliott)

56. Car 16 at Thorpe Bay is already 36 years old, but it still looks fit for a few more thousand miles. The crew pause for their photo to be taken before using the trolley reverser and returning to Southend High Street. Unfortunately this tram was broken up barely a year later in 1939. (W.A.Camwell)

57. A last look at Thorpe Esplanade as car 66 draws up to catch a minute's rest before the next stage of its journey. The motorist could expect no hand signals from the motorman.(W.A.Camwell)

58. Toastrack car 40 was converted into what can be best termed a carnival "float" when it sailed up and down the front during the annual jollifications from 1929-31. The whole vessel was declared "unseaworthy" in 1932 and HMHS Carnival was scuttled! (R.Sims)

59. A cross bench car swings northward away from the sea front and our journey along the boulevards begins. (G.L.Gundry)

60. High noon in Thorpe Bay and a standard three window open top car passes carrying a very unseasonal advertisement. (G.L.Gundry)

4. The Boulevards - Southchurch

61. Southend was one of the first tramway undertakings in the country to make use of reserved tracks for tramways. The entrance to the private right of way at Thorpe serves to illustrate this new concept in town planning. (G.L.Gundry Coll.)

62. Some years later towards the end of the tramway era, a double deck car sways to a halt before rejoining the main carriageway. (R.J.Harley Coll.)

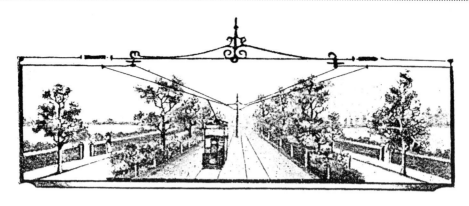

THORPE BAY.

THE new district of Thorpe Bay, which comprises about 500 acres, is situated on the east side of the Borough, extending as far as the boundary of the Urban District of Shoeburyness. There is a convenient Railway Station with accommodation for both passengers and goods traffic.

There is a well laid out and properly equipped golf course at 18 holes in practically the centre of the district, with a convenient and commodious club house.

Large sums of money have been spent in the construction of sea walls and promenades, pleasure grounds, and the laying out of roads on the new building estates, and the erection of good-class houses is proceeding rapidly.

The Southend Corporation have already extended their tramways to the south end of Thorpe Hall Avenue, which runs north and south through practically the centre of the district. They are extending their tramways throughout the whole length of this Avenue, and from the northern end along Southchurch Road to connect with their existing tramways near the "White Horse" Inn.

The scheme for this portion of the tramways is somewhat novel. It provides for the double line tramway track being laid in the centre of a strip of land at least 100 feet in width. On either side of the tramway track there will be a plantation of trees and shrubs and on either side of this plantation a carriage road and footway, so that there will be a boulevard extending from the sea front at Southend through Thorpe Hall Avenue and along Southchurch Road to the "White Horse" Inn, a distance of nearly two miles. Part of the routes, viz., from Southchurch Church to Bournes Green, is now in operation.

When this work has been completed the Corporation electric cars will follow a circular route, $1\frac{1}{2}$ miles of which will consist of marine esplanade and two miles of boulevard.

Extract from the *STANDARD GUIDE* of 1914.

63. Housing development has already started in this view of Thorpe Hall Boulevard taken around 1914. (G.L.Gundry Coll.)

64. It was said that the boulevard route never made a profit and voices were raised in the council chamber to have the line curtailed in winter. The tramways department paid the wages of six gardeners and when this task was transferred to the parks department, the service paid! Whatever the merits of this argument, as can be seen from this view, the corporation's budding "Capability Browns" certainly tried hard. (R.J.Harley Coll.)

65. Looking more like a setting for "Midsummer Night's Dream" than a tram route, car 53 emerges through dappled sunlight into a woodland glade. (G.L.Gundry Coll.)

66. Many of the mature trees were preserved on the construction of the tramways and clearances were sometimes very tight between trams and tree trunks. At Southchurch a large walnut tree was preserved in the garden of a demolished post office and only six inches separated it from the bright green paintwork of the passing tramcars! (G.L.Gundry Coll.)

67. Clearly to be seen in this view of car 41 are the handles of the shutters which could be lowered in inclement weather. (G.L.Gundry Coll.)

68. Postcards showing the boulevards tramway have an inviting look about them and one wonders what sort of tourist attraction the ride would have made had it survived into the post war years. In this picture taken in the last summer of operation, car 41 rocks and sways on the worn rails. (W.A.Camwell)

69. Not much room to spare as cars 57 and 24 squeeze past the photographer. (W.A.Camwell)

70. The tracks have just been laid and ballasted and car 28 halts in the middle of the Essex countryside for the moment to be preserved on film. Later views show that grass seed was sown between the rails to give a lawn like quality. (G.L.Gundry Coll.)

71. Evidence here that conifers have been clipped and shaped to allow the passage of the tramcars. Only the outline of the house roof to the right of the tram intrudes on the bucolic nature of the scene. (R.J.Harley Coll.)

72. Car 50 is almost brand new as it tackles the sharp bend from Thorpe Hall Boulevard into Southchurch Boulevard. Here at Bournes Green in this 1921 photo there are still as yet very few signs of habitation. (Lens of Sutton)

73. Spring is about to burst on Bournes Green; new foliage is appearing on the oaks and elms carefully preserved around the new tramway. A lone cyclist takes a pause for reflection as the motorman waits on the platform of his tram. (G.L.Gundry Coll.)

74. A 1938 view of the tramway reservation and the service has but a few weeks left before the wires are taken down and the rails ripped up and sold for scrap. The thick cables fed power into the overhead trolley wires. (W.A.Camwell)

76. The date is 30th July 1913, the opening day of service on this track and in this posed photo note that the trolley has already been turned for the journey back to Southend. (G.L.Gundry Coll.)

75. Our trip continues in the direction of the town centre. Car 6 waits on the edge of the shot; we can see that the new tramway has been built behind the old roadside hedgerow and field boundary. (G.L.Gundry Coll.)

77. Another opening day scene which appeared in the "Southend Graphic." Traffic Supt. Jack Daniels is at the controls of car 7 which had been newly rebuilt; some years later this car was relegated to serve as breakdown car 1. (J.H.Price Coll.)

78. A circular tour tram filled to capacity approaches Bournes Green. The dark green fleet livery must have blended in well with the local surroundings. (G.L.Gundry Coll.)

79. Looking towards Bournes Green car 12
speeds along the well laid tracks. The border
to the left of the tram was not planted out until
after the World War I. (G.L.Gundry Coll.)

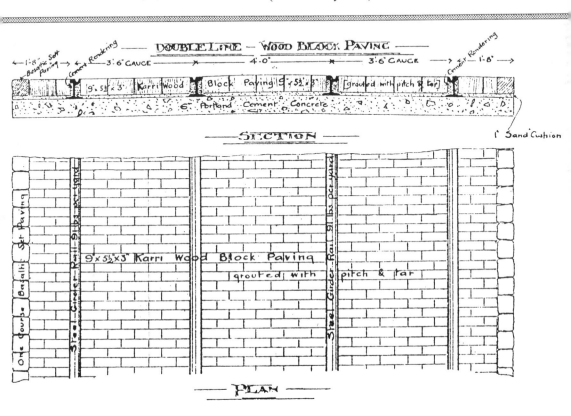

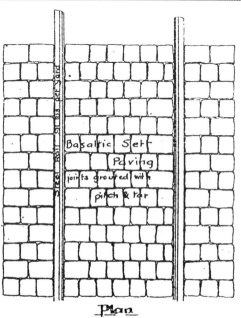

Steel Rail 90 lbs per Yard

Basaltic Sett
Paving
joints grouted with
pitch & tar

Plan

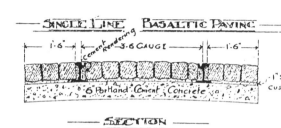

SINGLE LINE   BASALTIC PAVING

1·6" — cement Rendering — 3·6 GAUGE — 1·6"

6" Portland Cement Concrete

1" Sc
cush

SECTION

80. Taken from the top deck of a tram going the other way, car 41 catches the sun as the flags affixed to poles on the car roof flutter in the summer breeze. (C.Carter)

81. We reach Southchurch and with Hamstel Road in the background, car 44 in its final livery prepares to reverse on the crossover for the return to Leigh. (D.W.K.Jones)

E 5701
SOUTHEND-ON-SEA
CORPORATION TRAMWAYS.

Leigh-on-Sea Section.

| High Street to Leigh-on-Sea | Leigh-on-Sea to High Street |

EXCHANGE TICKET

To be given in exchange for a Return Ticket and NOT to be GIVEN OR TAKEN FOR MONEY.

This Ticket is available for One Journey on this Car only. It must be punched in the presence of the Passenger opposite the section on which the Passenger is entitled to travel and must be shown on demand.

Issued subject to the Bye-laws.

O 0766

SOUTHEND-ON-SEA
CORPORATION TRAMWAYS.

LEIGH-ON-SEA SECTION.

OUT.	FARE	IN.
High Street to Chalk-well Park	**3 d.**	Leigh-on-Sea to The Plough
The Plough to Leigh-on-Sea.	This ticket must be punched opposite the Section on which the Passenger is entitled to travel, and must be shown on demand.	Chalk-well Park to High Street.
LUGGAGE.		LUGGAGE.

Issued subject to the Bye-laws.

H 9314

SOUTHEND-ON-SEA
CORPORATION TRAMWAYS.

LEIGH-ON-SEA SECTION

OUT.	FARE	IN.
(Town L.T. & S. Rly. Stn.) to Chalkwell Park	**1 D**	Leigh-on-Sea to The Plough
The Plough to Leigh-on-Sea	This Ticket must be punched opposite the Section on which the Passenger is entitled to travel and must be shown on demand.	Chalkwell Park to Town (L.T. & S. Rly. Stn.)
LUGGAGE		LUGGAGE

Issued subject to the Bye-laws.

82. A lady with a shopping basket stands next to car 24, which is about to return to town. Behind the tram at the start of the reserved track, a couple of kids sit on a homemade soap box trolley. A bus registered HJ 1387 trundles off into the countryside along what would later become the Southend bound carriageway. Much of the charm of a more leisurely way of life is apparent on this summer's day decades ago. (G.L.Gundry Coll.)

83. At Southchurch we end our tour of Southend's tramways. The widespread use of the motor car in this 1938 picture has resulted in traffic lights being necessary to protect the road junction. Soon the trams will be a memory at this location and the centre strips on the boulevards will no longer echo to the swish of the trolley and the rhythm of the wheels on the rails. (W.A.Camwell)

5. Rolling Stock

Southend-on-Sea Corporation Tramways ran a varied fleet of both four and eight wheel cars. The depot workers and coachbuilders performed miracles of "make do and mend" whereby many trams were rebuilt with top covers and new windscreens. This philosophy was unfortunately only too typical of many British undertakings where the money was not forthcoming to renew the fleet regularly with modern vehicles. Certainly within the restrictions imposed by the narrow 3ft. 6ins./1067mm. track gauge much was achieved. The tram fleet was always painted in various shades of green and some of the important livery changes will be noted in the following photos. The motor buses and trolleybuses of the undertaking ended up in a pleasant, if unstriking, light blue shade.

CARS 1-10 Built by Brush in 1901 as four wheel open top cars on 5ft. 6ins. wheelbase Brill 21E trucks. Cars 1 and 2 were renumbered 11 and 12 in 1904. Cars 4, 7, 9 and 10 were all reconstructed in 1910-13.

CARS 11-12 Built by Brush in 1901 and subsequently renumbered 13 and 14 in 1904. They were eight wheel, open top cars on Brill 22E trucks; they received top covers in 1927.

CARS 13-14 Built by Brush in 1901, these two were single deck cars on 5ft. 6ins. wheelbase Brill 21E trucks. Both trams were rebuilt as open top, uncanopied double deckers in 1907-09.

CARS 15-17 Built by Brush in 1902 as eight wheel, uncanopied, open top cars, they were fitted with Brush maximum traction trucks and they were top covered in 1927.

CARS 18-22 Built by Milnes in 1904 as open top, bogie cars, they were all top covered in 1925. Supplied with Brill 22E trucks.

CARS 23-25 Built at Preston by UEC in 1909 as open top, bogie cars on MG maximum traction trucks. They were top covered in 1925.

CARS 26-31 Built by Brush in 1910 as four wheel, open top cars, they remained in this state until scrapped in 1934-39.

CARS 3, 5, 8, 11 These were replacement open top bodies mounted on reconditioned trucks; all were scrapped in 1934-37.

CARS 33-36 Built by Brush in 1912 as open top cars on four wheel radial trucks.

CARS 37-39 Built by Brush in 1912 as four wheel open top cars, their radial trucks were later exchanged for Burnley maximum traction bogies and the cars were fitted with top covers in 1925. Platform vestibule windscreens were added later.

CARS 40-43 The first three cars were delivered by Brush in 1914 and car 43 followed in 1921. They were cross bench, toastrack, single deck cars for the circular tour; they were said to be based on Canadian prototypes. Cars 40-42 were temporarily converted to enclosed saloon cars in 1916-19. Car 40 was rebuilt as an illuminated tram in 1929. All were mounted on Peckham P25 bogies. When space was short in the depot these cars would be stored on unelectrified track leading to the corporation loading pier; here they were moved around by means of a jumper cable attached to the overhead on the sea front.

CARS 44-55 Built by Brush in 1921 as eight wheel, top covered cars, most were later given platform vestibules. They ran on Peckham P25 trucks.

CARS 56-61 Built by English Electric on Burnley maximum traction trucks, these cars were delivered in 1923 and they all subsequently received windscreens.

COAL TRAMS

CARS 1A-3A These were constructed in 1914-15 on four wheel trucks salvaged from earlier cars. They were coal hopper wagons and were sent for scrap in 1931-32.

SECONDHAND TRAMS

CARS 62-65 Built by Hurst Nelson for Middlesbrough in 1921, they were covered top, open balconied, vestibuled, bogie cars mounted on Brill 22E trucks. They were acquired by Southend in 1934 and had to be regauged from Middlesbrough's unusual 3ft. 7ins. track gauge.

CARS 66-68 Built by Brush in 1919-1920 for Accrington, they were fully vestibuled, all enclosed eight wheel double deckers running on Brush maximum traction trucks. They came to Southend in 1934 and also had to be regauged. Accrington, like most of its North Lancashire neighbours, used a 4ft. track gauge.

84. Car 5 of the original fleet was scrapped in 1911. It is seen here with olive green rocker panels and dashes; the waist panels, window surrounds and stair stringers were painted in a lighter shade of sage green. Lettering was in gold. (G.L.Gundry Coll.)

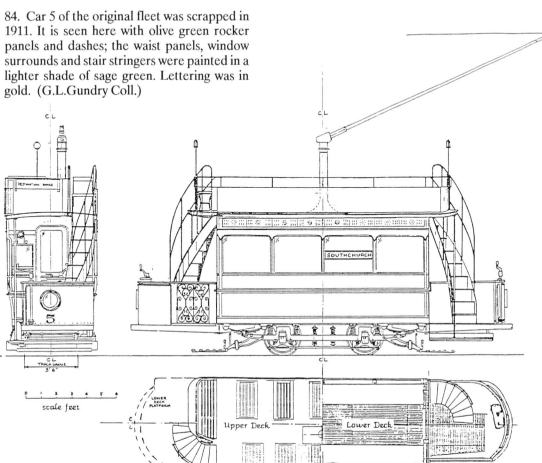

85. This photo appeared in the "Southend Graphic" under the headline. "Transforming a tramcar..The engineers dept. has converted some of the original small trams from 38 to 62 seats at a cost of £200 each." Car 6 shown here was the only one rebuilt like this with extra bulkheads, the rest were cut in the middle and a large window section inserted. (C.L.Rayner Coll.)

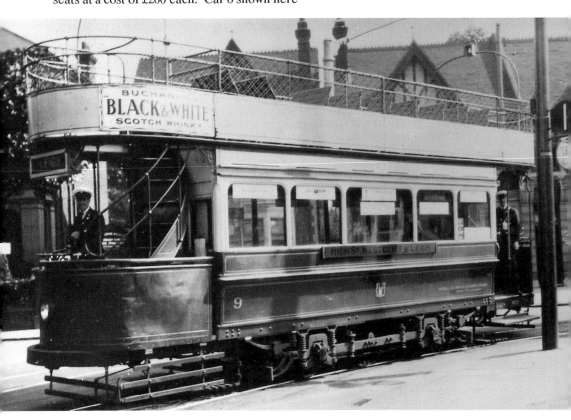

86. Car 9 was rebuilt in 1912-13 and the wheelbase of the truck increased to 8ft. (G.L.Gundry Coll.)

87. A close-up of car 10 after rebuilding with a lengthened lower saloon and platform canopies. (R.Sims)

88. Car 16 pictured in its final state wearing the medium green and ivory livery. (M.J.O'Connor)

89. Car 17 still in open top state with a dented dash in need of a repaint. Note the bell by the motorman's left hand. (R.Sims)

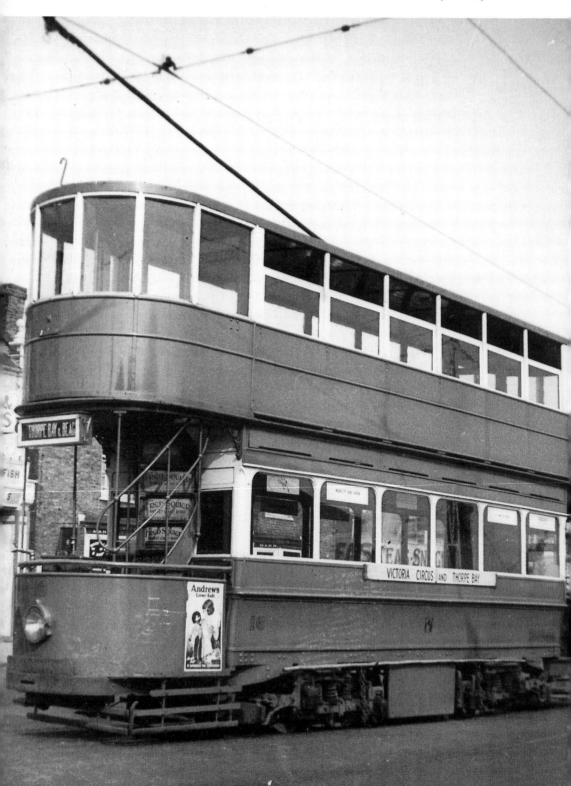

90. Car 20 in 1939 in the final livery.
(D.A.Thompson)

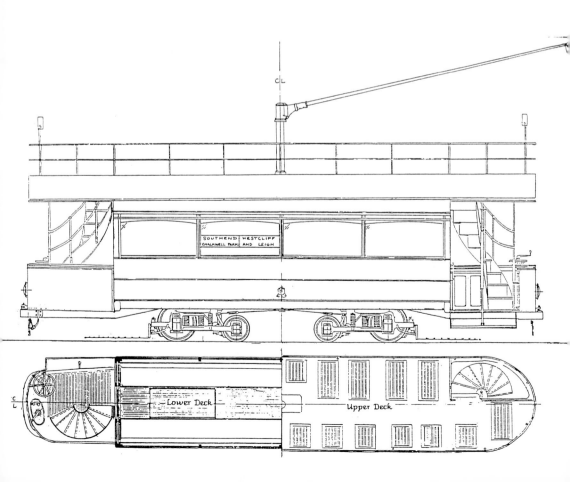

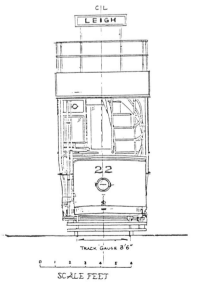

91. A contrast to the previous picture. This shows car 21 in early condition in the two tone green livery. (G.L.Gundry Coll.)

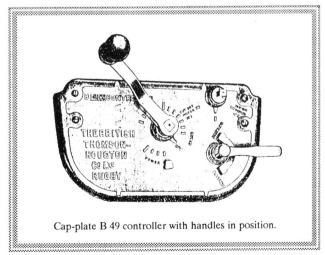

Cap-plate B 49 controller with handles in position.

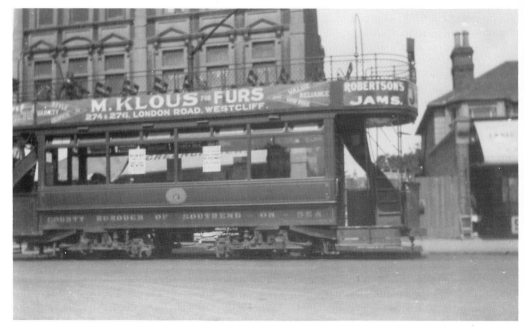

92   One of the 23-25 series cars in 1922. The
borough coat of arms is now displayed on the
waist panel on a light green oval background.
(G.L.Gundry)

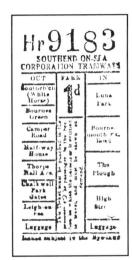

←

93. Car 24 demonstrates the additions of the reconstruction programme: a new enclosed top deck, new platform vestibules and a new livery. Inside the seating in both saloons was also improved. (D.A.Thompson)

94. In 1911 car 26 was retrucked on a Peckham P21 with an 8ft. wheelbase in an attempt to improve the riding qualities of the four wheel cars. (Tramway and Railway World)

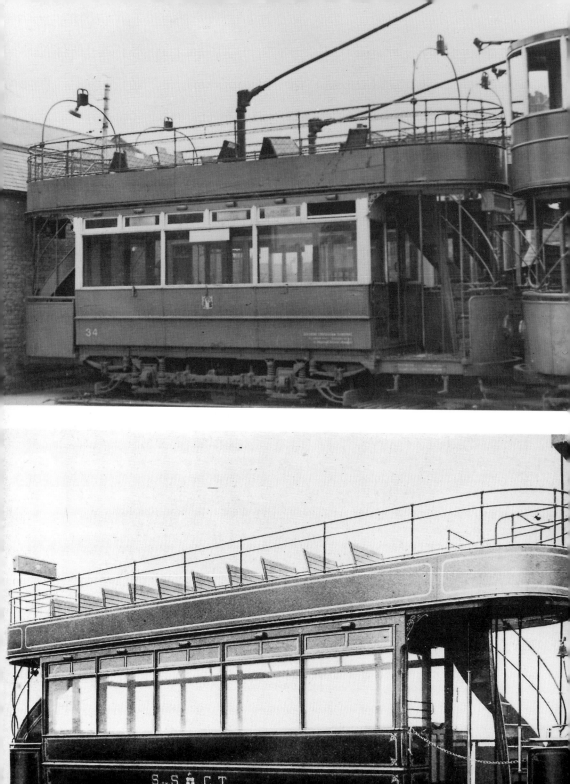
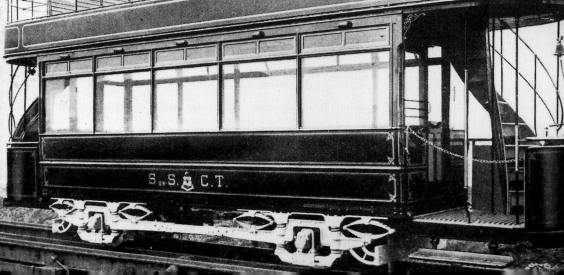

95. Car 34 dumped outside the depot awaiting the final round up! Note the elegant arched lamp supports on the top deck. (C.L.Rayner)

97. In its final guise, car 37 looks more conventional; it is seen here in 1939. (D.A.Thompson)

96. This view of car 37 shows the Peckham single axle radial truck with 13ft. 6ins. wheelbase and 22ft. spring base. In practice these trucks were not satisfactory and they were replaced in 1925 by Burnley maximum traction bogies. In 1916 this car was in an accident and it ran for two years with one dash painted grey. (Tramway and Railway World)

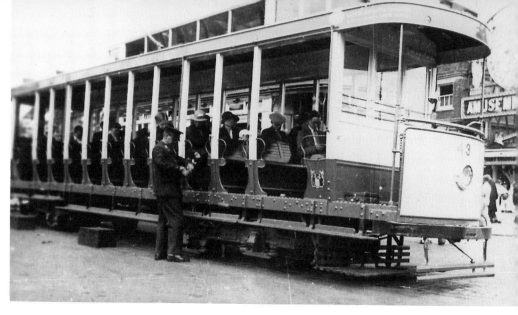

98. Toastrack car 43 is painted in ivory and medium green with the coat of arms on the waist panel by the front seat.
(National Tramway Museum)

99. This is the official photo produced by the Brush Company of Loughborough; the background has been painted out and the livery details on the tram touched up. However, it is still a handsome car and the dark green livery must have contrasted well with the cream top deck lined out in black and the maroon trucks and lifeguards.
(Brush Company)

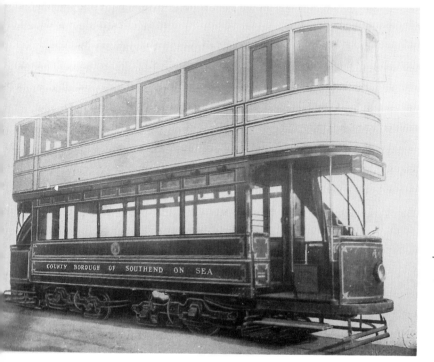

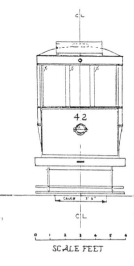

SCALE FEET

00. One of the 44-55 series cars bears publicity
or a well known local trader. R.A.Jones and
Sons were noted as "the" Essex jewellers; their
shop in the High Street used to advertise

"Presents from 1/- (5p) to £100 from the
Largest Stock in the Eastern Counties!" The
date is 1922. (G.L.Gundry)

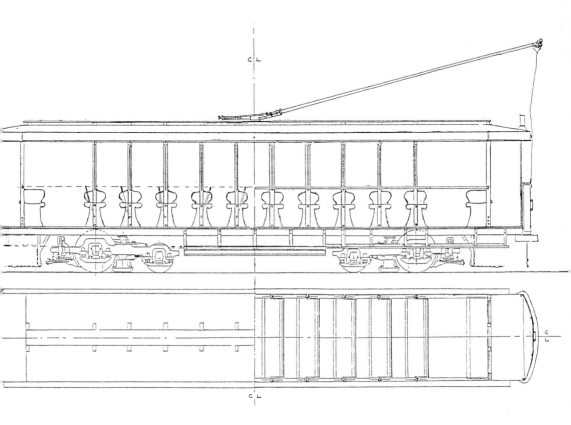

101. Car 53 on a warm day exhibiting the rather ugly syle of windscreen which was fitted to some of these cars. (M.J.O'Connor)

103. Car 60 was one of the last batch of t delivered new to Southend. Here we see the end of its career. (W.A.Camwell)

104. The only open balcony cars in the were those acquired from Middlesbroug 1934. Car 64, pictured here, had a short li its new home, being sent for scrap in (W.A.Camwell)

102. Car 54 shows minor paint differences t the previous photo. Notice the top of th windscreen and the rail above the windows ha been painted ivory. An anti-climbing meta plate has been fixed to the fender of the tram (D.A.Thompson)

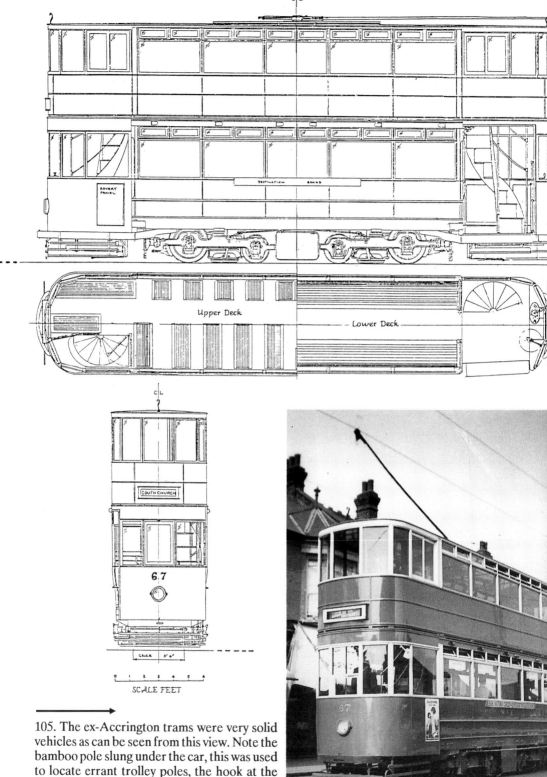

Upper Deck

Lower Deck

SOUTH CHURCH

6 7

GAUGE 3' 6"

0 1 2 3 4 5 6
SCALE FEET

105. The ex-Accrington trams were very solid
vehicles as can be seen from this view. Note the
bamboo pole slung under the car, this was used
to locate errant trolley poles, the hook at the
end fitting neatly through the metal ring which
can just be seen hanging from the swivel trolley
head of car 67. (M.J.O'Connor)

106. No, the men in white coats haven't arrived to escort visiting tram fans to happier pastures! In fact car 27 has been decorated for carnival week and the crew are collecting for local hospital charities. (R.Sims)

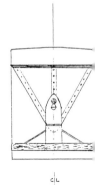

107. Pushing the boat out took on another meaning for the tramway staff summoned to rescue HMHS Carnival, a.k.a. car 40, in its twilight years when occasional electrical failures and an unsafe body demanded all hands on deck! (R.Sims)

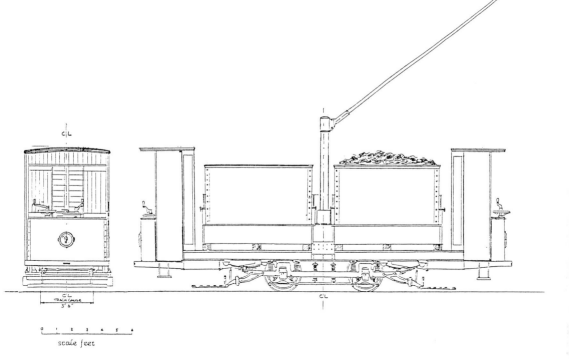

scale feet

108. Car 1 dressed overall as the Fleet Tram is seen here in the depot yard in 1909. All this was in aid of HM Fleet Review off Southend; the message on the side reads "Welcome To Our Sailors." (C.L.Rayner)

109. The coal tram is basking unnoticed by the general public. All three cars were pressed into service in 1915 and went about their unglamorous occupations until the early 1930s when the corporation switched from steam to diesel generators in the power station. A fourth coal tram body was built, but was never used. The paint scheme was a utilitarian plain, flat grey. (D.W.K.Jones)

110. One of the 200 kilowatt generating sets is seen here. The engines were of the vertical compound Corliss type, with cylinders 14ins. and 31ins. in diameter and the normal speed was 110 revolutions per minute. (Tramway and Railway World)

6. Finale

111. "For whom the bell tolls." The funeral rites are about to begin for the last circular tour on 6th July 1938. Buses then took over the service and no more would the plaintive sound of tramcar bells be heard as they swayed along grass covered tracks. (C.L.Rayner)

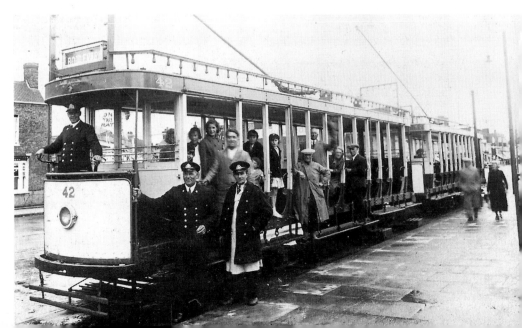

112. What to do with unwanted tramcars? Drag them off the rails, leave them outside the depot and wait for a buyer to collect. (C.L.Rayner)

113. After the demise of the tramways electric traction lingered on in Southend in the form of the trolleybus system. Here is ex-Teeside bus 140 seen in August 1948. However, pressure on the corporation for an integrated transport network based solely on motor buses caused the departure of the last trolleybus on 28th October 1954. (S.E.Letts)

7. Pier Tramway

114. The first tramway along the pier opened for business in the early 1850s. The date on this card is wrong and the view was taken sometime after 1885. Two members of the tramway staff are dressed as jolly matelots to impart a nautical flavour to the trot over the waves. (J.H.Price Coll.)

Steamer service shown in Bradshaw for July 1906.

THE SOUTHEND ELECTRICAL TRAMWAY.

The interesting features of this tramway are the despatch with which the work was carried out, and the means by which this was accomplished, by using material from stock. The Southend Local Board, which is following the example of the enterprise of other watering places in spending money on local improvements, recently replaced the long wooden pier by an iron struc-

Crompton Dynamo; 150 amperes, 200 volts.

track is of 3ft. 6in. gauge, the rails being of Vignolle's type. The conductor is laid about 12in. from one of the rails, and 1in. below the level of the rail tops. The rails are used for the return. The motor is a stock pattern; it is speeded down by simple spur gearing as 3 to 1. At both ends of the car are handles for starting and reversing, with an ordinary brake. While 20 miles an hour can be attained, the car runs generally at 12 to 14 miles an hour, the trip being made in three or four minutes, instead of 15 minutes with horse cars. The

current is collected by rubbing contacts designed by Mr. Chamen, to whom, with Mr. Scott Moncrieff, special credit is due for the prompt execution of the work. Dr. Hopkinson, as consulting engineer to the Local Board, expressed great satis-

End View of Car, three-quarters of a mile down the pier.

ture, at a cost of about £80,000. To keep things up to date, it was decided to furnish the new pier with an electrical tramway. Tenders were invited, and the contract was secured by Messrs. Crompton and Co. Three-quarters of a mile of track was laid the car built and fitted; a horizontal compound engine by Davey Paxman, with a boiler of locomotive type, was provided, and the connecting cables were laid so smartly that the tramway was at work in six weeks, and succeeded in earning on Bank Holiday the satisfactory "traffic receipts" which we mentioned last week. The dynamo is of the Crompton standard type, and is compound-wound for 150 amperes at 200 volts. The conductor on the pier is of the ordinary 1in. by ·134in. copper strip, which is used for street mains; and the supports, insulators, and straining gear have been taken from stock, and are identical with those used in 30 miles of streets in Kensington, Belgravia, and Notting Hill. The insulators are placed at intervals of 15 yards, and straining gear with volute springs are placed at every 85 yards, The

Car travelling at sixteen miles an hour.

faction with the work, which is much appreciated by the residents. The power required for propelling the car is considerably below that which was expected; and Messrs. Crompton and Co. hope to make measurements of the tractive force, and intend to publish the results of their experiments.

115. Between decks on the pier and one four-car set is maintaining the winter operation. These vehicles were built by AC Cars of Thames Ditton, Surrey, and delivered in 1949; they ran on Maley and Taunton trucks of 14ft. 6ins wheelbase. (J.H.Price)

117. January 1949 and a lonely winter car braves the cold sea mists. At this time of the year the colour light signals were switched off and only one track was used on the one engine in steam principle. (J.H.Meredith)

116. The old and the new on 11th June 1949, the car on the right dates from before World War I. (J.H.Meredith)

118. Some idea of the summer popularity of the pier tramway can be gained by this view of a seven car set negotiating the scissors crossover in August 1948. (S.E.Letts)

119. One of the winter combination cars is caught by the camera at the halfway siding in 1922. The pier was widened and improved in 1927-29 and double track was installed throughout. (G.L.Gundry)

120. This seven car set consists of control trailer, closed trailer, open trailer, powered car, control trailer, open trailer and finally control trailer. Obviously this combination could be separated to cope with varying traffic demands. (D.A.Thompson)

121. Before catching the boat to sail away from Southend, we cast one backward glance at the pier in its Edwardian heyday. (G.L.Gundry Coll.)